The Zodiac
Kama
Sutra

*A Guide to the
Sexology of Astrology*

Lydia Levine

summersdale

THE ZODIAC KAMA SUTRA

Text by Lucy York

An Hachette UK Company
www.hachette.co.uk

Summersdale Publishers
Part of Octopus Publishing Group Limited
Carmelite House
50 Victoria Embankment
LONDON
EC4Y 0DZ
UK

www.summersdale.com

Printed and bound in China

ISBN: 978-1-83799-382-6

Substantial discounts on bulk quantities of Summersdale books are available to corporations, professional associations and other organizations. For details contact general enquiries: telephone: +44 (0) 1243 771107 or email: enquiries@summersdale.com.

Contents

Introduction

Welcome to *The Zodiac Kama Sutra*. Many, many years ago, one very saucy author and his collection of very bendy friends got together, and the result was the ancient erotic text known as the *Kama Sutra*. Well, maybe it didn't happen exactly like that, but in any case, a wealth of sex positions was recorded. It is from this iconic book about living and loving well that the humble tome you now hold in your hands draws inspiration, combining ancient sexpertise with the wonders of astrology to pinpoint exactly which sexy shenanigans will work best for your zodiac sign.

In the following pages, you will find overviews of each star sign's personality; use them to gain further insight about yourself and your partner or love interest. These are accompanied by sex tips and positions relevant to each sign. Use them for inspiration, but don't be afraid to experiment and find what works best for you and your lover. As always in matters of love, communication is key, so check in with your partner along the way. With a few tweaks here and there, most of the tips and positions can be adapted for whatever magical combination of genders and sexual preference makes up your unique love duo. Whether you're attempting The Plough position, experimenting with sex toys or trying role play for the first time, the most important thing is to do whatever feels good – and have fun!

How to Use This Book

This book is divided into 12 chapters, one for each sign of the zodiac, from Aries through to Pisces. Each chapter begins with a personality overview, giving insights into the key traits and tendencies of people who have that zodiac sign as their sun sign. This is followed by an exploration of how the signs show up in love and relationships. There are then summaries of the rising star sign and the Moon in each star sign – see page 12 for a guide to how this works. Next comes the juicy part: each chapter contains three pages of sex tips and positions for the sun sign, and a sex position for each of the rising and moon signs. In the sex position descriptions, the terms "active" and "passive" partner are used. The active partner is the one doing most of the physical work, while the passive partner usually has a less active role. You can use this book to learn more about yourself and what works best in bed for you, as well as for your partner or any potential love interest.

The Basics of Astrology

Maybe you are familiar with astrology from the columns that appear in magazines and newspapers or online – fun little paragraphs that tell you whether you'll be lucky in love this month or if it's time to seek a new career opportunity. Well, there is so much more to astrology than that. Western astrology is an all-encompassing study of human experience, based on the concept that everybody's personality is informed by the date, time and place of their birth. These factors determine your sun, moon and rising placements.

Astrology offers deep insight into our personal motivation and behaviour and helps us understand our relationships with others. It doesn't describe your personality in certain terms, but rather the *potential* for characteristics to come to the fore.

Most importantly, astrology can help you to learn more about yourself. Understanding why you act in a certain way and acknowledging your fears or desires helps you to feel at greater ease with yourself and the world. It makes you feel more whole as a person, and more confident as a lover and romantic partner.

The 12 Signs of the Zodiac

The 12 signs of the zodiac correspond with the 12 constellations that the Sun, Moon and planets travel most often "through" (or appear to travel through) on a path known as the ecliptic. The connection between the real path of these celestial bodies and the path mapped on astrological charts is approximate, smoothed out for ease of measurement.

The word "zodiac" means "circle of animals", which is reflected in the symbols that represent each astrological sign, as shown on the opposite page. Each sign has a sun, moon and rising variation. Although there is a strong thread connecting these three variations – for example a Pisces Sun and a Pisces Rising may both be dreamers – the celestial object in each sign will impact the strength of these characteristics. To calculate your sun, moon and rising signs, enter your time, date and place of birth into an online zodiac calculator (see page 125).

Aries
21 March–
19 April

Taurus
20 April–
20 May

Gemini
21 May–
20 June

Cancer
21 June–
22 July

Leo
23 July–
22 August

Virgo
23 August–
22 September

Libra
23 September–
22 October

Scorpio
23 October–
21 November

Sagittarius
22 November–
21 December

Capricorn
22 December–
19 January

Aquarius
20 January–
18 February

Pisces
19 February–
20 March

Elemental Types

Each zodiac sign falls under one of four elemental types: earth, air, water and fire. The elements each carry their own traits. These, combined with the influence of the stars, form the basis of your personality.

Earth:
Taurus, Virgo, Capricorn
Key characteristics: grounded, cautious, prizes stability

Air:
Gemini, Libra, Aquarius
Key characteristics: outgoing, idealistic, intellectual, goes with the flow

Water:
Cancer, Scorpio, Pisces
Key characteristics: intuitive, empathetic, sensitive

Fire:
Aries, Leo, Sagittarius
Key characteristics: active, spontaneous, playful

Love Compatibility

You will get on better in love with certain zodiac signs than others because you share similar traits and qualities, or because they mirror back to you what you need to explore in yourself.

Fire signs: Aries, Leo, Sagittarius
Compatible with air signs
Enthusiastic, spontaneous and active, fire signs get bored with too much practical planning (Earth) and are uncomfortable with emoting (Water). But they can learn by being more analytical (Air).

Earth signs: Taurus, Virgo, Capricorn
Compatible with water signs
Practical, stable and conservative earth signs are suspicious of too much spontaneity (Fire) or lack of practicality (Air). They empathize with the emotive side of water signs.

Air signs: Gemini, Libra, Aquarius
Compatible with fire signs
Intellectual, versatile and analytical, air signs feel burdened by water signs' neediness and irritated by

Earth's slowness to take action. They can learn from the fire signs' assertiveness.

Water signs: Cancer, Scorpio, Pisces
Compatible with earth signs
Intuitive, emotional and imaginative, water signs distrust fire signs' directness and dislike Air's tendency to intellectualize. They understand Earth's need for structure and deliberation.

Sun, Rising and Moon Signs: What They Are

Sun: You are probably most familiar with your sun sign, which is defined by the position of the Sun in the sky when you were born. Your sun sign represents your core traits – the ones that drive you and that you keep returning to. And yet, it doesn't show the whole story. Look to your rising and moon signs for more nuance and a fuller picture of your personality.

Rising: Your rising sign reflects the location of the constellation on the eastern horizon at the time of your birth. The location and date of your birth impacts this. Your rising sign is often the face that you present most outwardly to the world. It's a more curated, inner version of yourself that you choose when to show and who you show it to. But that doesn't make it any less authentic, in your rising sign, you will often find the elements of yourself that you admire and would like to be known for. Some people feel that their rising-sign self is their "true" self.

Moon: Your moon sign is determined by the location of the moon at the time you were born. It's most deeply connected to your emotional nature, so you might notice that the traits you find in your moon sign reflect the way your emotions flow and the way you prefer to express them. Your moon sign contains the key to the ways you need to be emotionally nourished in order to grow. You'll also notice that your instinctual reactions to situations reflect your moon sign nature.

Aries

Dates: 21 March–19 April

Zodiac symbol: The ram
Ruling planet: Mars
Element: Fire
Body hot spots: Head, eyes, face

Sun Sign: Personality Overview

Just like the ram, Aries are independent and determined. And, boy, do they like to be in charge – whether that's at work or in the bedroom! In fact, they are natural-born leaders. Since they enjoy making the rules so much, they can find it a little difficult to take direction from others. However, their restless, vibrant energy and enthusiasm makes them hard to resist.

Aries people are brave and tackle any obstacles head-on. Above all, they love spontaneity and adventure, which, where love is concerned, can lead to a lot of fun! When it comes to money, they typically like to spend, spend, spend, so if you enjoy receiving extravagant presents, an Aries could be the one for you. Unfortunately, this preference for short-term excitement over careful budgeting can also translate into a dislike of commitment in relationships. Having said that, if you want passion, you've come to the right place. Aries fall in love easily and always wear their heart on their sleeve, making them easy to fall for.

Love and Relationships

Given their inherently passionate nature, Aries people want someone who can match their enthusiasm in love. An Aries will not want to engage in too much practical planning, and they won't want to talk about their feelings all the time. What they will do is flirt outrageously and keep you on your toes. They crave adventure and can get bored easily – so when it comes to dates, think white-water rafting rather than cosy nights in. In between all the fun, they do need intelligent conversation and witty banter to keep them interested.

When it comes to sex... well, be prepared to use your imagination and give anything a try. In the bedroom, they love spontaneity, mixing things up with different positions. They also love a bit of rough-and-ready action – as long as their partner is down for that, too – but they lack the patience for Tantric sex.

They are best matched with Leo, Sagittarius and Libra, while liaisons with Taurus and Pisces usually don't end well.

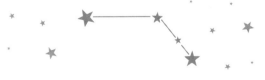

Rising Sign: Overview

An Aries Rising person's instinct is always to act first, ask questions later. They will jump straight in and tackle things head-on, without considering how things will work out. This can lead to some, er... rather awkward situations. On the other hand, their candidness and courage are disarming, so they often get what they want. It also means that they tend to have a direct way of communicating what they want in the bedroom.

Moon Sign: Overview

The Aries sign is the first in the zodiac, and Moon in Aries people have a tendency to put themselves first. Let's just say they are experts at getting their own needs met. Their natural impulsiveness means they are quick to feel love but also anger. They are passionate by nature, and when they love, they really give it their all. Aries Moon people are honest and straightforward, if a little lacking in tact at times. They can learn from their mistakes, though, and can work at holding back on their impulses.

Sun Sign Aries: Sitting Lotus

Aries are born to lead, and of course, that applies in the bedroom. This face-to-face position creates intimacy and connection and also provides the opportunity for plenty of dirty talk – or commands. It can be adapted for any gender combination and works equally well for vaginal and anal penetration, or even no penetration at all. You can really get creative with it, which is perfect for spontaneous Aries!

The person who will be penetrating, if that's your thing, sits in a cross-legged position, while the active partner (yup, that's you, Aries!) straddles them on top, wrapping their legs around the other. The partner on top controls the speed and flavour of the movement. Best suited to long, slow, soulful lovemaking sessions, which passionate Aries will love.

Sun Sign Aries:
Sensual Head Massage

The Aries sun sign corresponds with the head and face, so what better way to get your Aries partner in the mood than with a sensual head massage? To set the mood, dim the lights or light some candles. Sit on the bed and invite your partner to sit between your legs, with eyes closed, facing away.

Start the massage with the shoulders, use soothing, firm strokes, and progress to the upper back. Gradually extend up along the neck. Move onto the scalp, making slow circular movements. Finally, use the thumbs to massage from the centre of the forehead to the outer edges.

Using an aromatherapy oil such as ylang-ylang, jasmine or patchouli can really enhance the senses. Pop a few drops in some carrier oil and add a drop to your palms. Rub your palms together and hold them in front of your partner's nose so that they can inhale the aroma.

Sun Sign Aries:
It's All About the Eyes

The eyes are key for Aries, and you can have a lot of fun together with a blindfold. Although, given Aries like to be in control, it may be their partner wearing it, while Aries lavishes them with passion. Here are a few ideas:

- Waft various delicious foods under the nose of your blindfolded partner and challenge them to guess what each is. If they guess right, they take a bite. If they are wrong, you can nibble on one of their body parts.

- Blindfold your partner and then lead them out of the bedroom...

- Both wear a blindfold and masturbate together. With your eyes covered, you can release your inhibitions and moans of pleasure.

- Blindfold your partner and tease their nipples with an ice cube.

Rising Sign Aries: The Plough

This is the perfect position for gung-ho Aries Rising. It's not for the faint-hearted – which Aries will love, because they are always ready for a challenge, and they have the stamina to pull it off.

The active partner stands near the edge of the bed, while the passive partner lies face down with their legs over the edge. The active partner steps between the passive partner's legs and raises them, so that the passive partner comes up onto their elbows and into a plank-like position. Grasping the passive partner's hips, the active partner can then penetrate or grind against their partner.

The active partner will have to get the pacing right so that things come to a head before they run out of stamina.

To make this more comfortable for the passive partner, pop a pillow beneath their elbows.

Moon Sign Aries:
Reverse Cowgirl/Cowboy

It's an oldie, but it's a goodie. Aries Moon will love the chance to get up on top and take the lead with this energetic position, which requires more quad strength than the regular cowgirl/cowboy. They can ensure their needs get met while giving their partner a jaw-dropping show.

The passive partner lies on their back with their legs together, while the active partner straddles them, facing away from their partner. If you're opting for penetration, now is the time for the passive partner to slide their way in. The rider then rocks back and forth in a tempo of their choosing while the passive partner enjoys the view.

Experiment with the angle until you feel comfortable. If the rider needs extra support, they can lean back with their hands either side of their partner's torso.

Taurus

Dates: 20 April–20 May

Zodiac symbol: The bull
Ruling planet: Venus
Element: Earth
Body hot spots: Neck, throat, ears

Sun Sign: Personality Overview

Ah, good old dependable, strong, patient Taurus. When a Taurus has a goal, they will focus unwaveringly on it – whether it's securing a new business deal or wooing a love interest. No matter what the obstacles, they will persevere. And that usually results in success, which means having a Taurus in your life can be pretty inspiring.

It can be challenging, too. For with their determination comes a certain amount of stubbornness. They don't like change, and they certainly won't be rushed into making any decisions. Neither do they give their hearts away easily – but when they do, they are in it for the long game.

Bulls love nothing more than a cosy, comfortable home, which is where they are happiest. But that's not to say they are dull – in fact, being ruled by Venus, the planet of harmony and beauty, Taureans are often artistic and talented individuals. So don't be surprised if you come home to an exotic flower arrangement created by your Taurean lover or find yourself being serenaded at sunset.

Love and Relationships

It can take a while for a Taurus to warm up, but once they commit, they are loyal and loving, and their relationships are usually long-lasting. They will do anything for the one they love.

Since Taureans don't adapt well to change, they get along best with someone who also appreciates routine and comfort. They find any unpredictability or insecurity a massive turn-off. Speaking of comfort: nobody appreciates good food and wine like a Taurean, so think long, romantic meals and weekends away to foodie locations.

Their penchant for indulging the senses extends to the bedroom, and they like to experiment with all of them – from the taste of chocolate on warm skin to the touch of silky knickers, and from the sound of you whispering dirty secrets to the scent of ylang-ylang oil on your nipples and the sight of you slowly undressing. Oh, and rumour has it that the Bull can go the distance.

Their best zodiac matches are Cancer, Scorpio and Virgo, while Leo and Aquarius should give them a wide berth.

Rising Sign: Overview

A person with Taurus Rising moves serenely through life. They're not in any hurry, and they especially like to take their time when it comes to making love. If you're lucky enough to get an invite to their home, expect to find a den of indulgent comfort, with soft cushions and sumptuous rugs to sink into together. They also enjoy the finer things in life, so post-coital snacks are likely to be high end. Connect with these creative souls through a shared love of art or music.

Moon Sign: Overview

Security is the key word for Moon in Taurus people. These calm folk are slow to react, but once they set a course or form an opinion, it's impossible to convince them otherwise. And, boy, do they love to plan. Their careful approach means that they take other people's feelings seriously and their take on romance tends to be traditional. Be warned, though, despite their calm exterior, Moon in Taurus folk can harbour resentment, eventually leading to an explosive outburst.

Sun Sign Taurus: Spooning

Taureans have a reputation for taking their time, easing themselves slowly into things – and this laid-back position is perfect for just that. Picture a lazy Sunday morning in a Taurean's cosy, luxurious bedroom, spooning your way into heavenly bliss together.

The passive partner lies curled on their side, while the active partner takes up the position of the big spoon, curling behind them. The active partner penetrates the passive partner or reaches around and pleases them with their hand – or both at once.

This position allows the active partner to stimulate a key erogenous zone on the back of their partner's neck. Try breathing softly on this sensitive spot, or, if you have facial hair and really want to drive them wild, gently scrape your chin back and forth.

Sun Sign Taurus: Deep Throat

The throat is one of the key areas of the body associated with Taurus, and this tip is specifically for Taureans who want to please a partner who has a penis. It can take some practice, so take your time and stop if either of you feels uncomfortable or if it is causing unwanted gagging.

Start by sensually smoothing lubrication over the penis. Next, get into position on your back on the bed with your mouth open, ready to receive your partner's penis. Guide it into your mouth, picking up a slow back-and-forth rhythm as you gradually ease it further in until it reaches the back of your throat. Breathe through your nose; take a break if you need to. Most importantly, relax and have fun.

Sun Sign Taurus: I'm All Ears

The ears are one of the key erogenous zones, and no star sign loves a tickle of the earlobe better than Taurus. Here are some ideas to get your Taurus tingling:

- Massage the earlobe with your thumb and index finger in a gentle circular motion.

- Blow gently into the ear to create a pleasurable, ticklish breeze, or whisper a few sexy sweet nothings.

- Kiss and flick the lobe and inner parts of the ear gently with your tongue.

Everyone responds differently to their ear being stimulated, so remember to check in with your partner about what works best for them. You might want to ask in advance before popping a tongue in – no one likes a surprise wet willy.

Rising Sign Taurus: Take a Break

Taurus ascending people are very fond of taking their sweet time at things, and never more so than when it comes to lovemaking. If something is pleasurable, then why not make it last as long as possible?

This position can be slotted into a lovemaking session to slow the pace down or bring you both back from the edge. Move from whichever position you have been using to lie side by side, facing one another. If you were using penetration, the penetrating partner should stay inside.

Intertwine your legs, press your chests together and kiss and touch each other sensually as your breathing slows. Stay like this as long as you want – or until you both can't wait any longer to shift things back up a gear.

Moon Sign Taurus: The Rocking Horse

Slow and careful Moon in Taurus folk will love this position in which both partners can feel comfortable and supported. Perfect for languid lovemaking sessions as you gaze into each other's eyes.

The passive partner sits, usually with their legs stretched out in front, with their arms behind to lean on for support. The active partner, who can be penetrated if you choose, straddles the passive partner, lowering themselves onto their lap. They can hold on to the passive partner for support if needed. The active partner moves in a bouncing or swaying motion, building up a rhythm that will rock you both into nirvana.

From their vantage point, the active partner can also caress or kiss the passive partner's neck – one of the key parts of the Taurean anatomy!

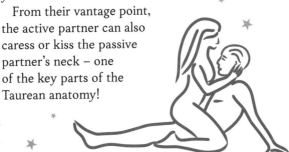

Gemini

Dates: 21 May–20 June

Zodiac symbol: The twins
Ruling planet: Mercury
Element: Air
Body hot spots: Hands, arms, lungs

Sun Sign: Personality Overview

Geminis are named after the twins Castor and Pollux in Greek mythology, so it should come as no surprise that they can display two very different sides to their personality and shift between them quickly. Cheerful and outgoing one minute, they can be moody and withdrawn the next, which means being with a Gemini can be a bit of a rollercoaster.

Geminis are curious, clever and adaptable, so they tend to have a lot of different projects on the go. And since they easily adapt to new surroundings and circumstances, they often love to travel. Life with a Gemini is never dull.

Quick-witted, light-hearted and ruled by loquacious Mercury, Geminis are talented communicators. They make excellent salespeople, pick up new languages fast and thrive in any situation where there are plenty of people to talk to. Because of this, Geminis tend to have loads of friends, and they have a gift for finding things in common with people. They can also be incorrigible flirts. Indeed, their love lives can be a colourful adventure!

Love and Relationships

Communication is important to Geminis, and never more so than in their romantic relationships. They need a partner who is open and honest and will regularly discuss their thoughts and feelings with them – otherwise they can end up jumping to their own conclusions, leading to misunderstandings and conflict. For Geminis, it's more about intellect than emotion when it comes to love. Big emotions can scare them, and they prefer to rationalize their feelings.

In the bedroom, Geminis love a bit of pillow talk. And they have no qualms about telling you what they want and how they want it. They are terrible teases between the sheets and will keep you wanting more. Gemini is a sign of change, so be prepared to change sexual positions frequently and try various locations. Though be aware: this also means that they have a tendency to change partners often.

Gemini vibes best with Sagittarius, Libra and Leo. Things don't usually end well when they get entangled with Taurus or Scorpio.

Rising Sign: Overview

Meeting a Gemini Rising for the first time can feel a bit like an interrogation, thanks to their curiosity and need to categorize the world. On the plus side, this means they are great at getting others to open up; but, as they are so busy talking, they can sometimes miss what's going on underneath the surface. They are very adaptable and aren't afraid to initiate change. One thing's for sure – you won't get bored in bed with a Gemini Rising.

Moon Sign: Overview

The duality of Gemini comes into play here. People who have a Gemini Moon can be attracted physically to people they may not be emotionally compatible with. Their sexual mood can be fickle, too, with what they desire changing abruptly.

A Gemini Moon person is witty, and they tend to be light-hearted when dealing with their own emotions. When dealing with others' emotions, they come at it from a purely intellectual level, which can make them seem superficial. But if you respect their need to be recognized as intelligent, you'll be on your way to capturing their heart.

Sun Sign Gemini: The Plain

Geminis will adore this cheeky little number, which also allows them to easily shift into other similarly orientated positions (a bit of low doggy or a sneaky rear oral, anyone?) or roll their partner into a completely different pose. As we know, Geminis do love to change things up.

The passive partner lies on their stomach with their legs pointing back and arms straight in front, slightly raising their torso. The active partner then gets on top of the passive partner with their legs either side. From here, the active partner can easily penetrate and/or reach around to caress the passive partner's breasts or nipples.

If the passive partner twists slightly, they can cast a naughty glance in the active partner's direction and exchange a bit of dirty talk – which chatty Geminis will love.

Sun Sign Gemini: Getting Handsy

The hands are one of the body hot spots for Gemini, so it's no surprise that many Geminis are good with their hands. Here are some ways Geminis can use their dexterous digits to set their partner's temperature rising:

- Take your partner's palm in your hand and, with the fingers of your other hand, lightly trace patterns across its surface. Extend the caresses up the wrist. Keep going until they can't take it anymore.

- Gently flick your partner's nipples with your thumbs.

- Give your mouth a helping hand during oral sex – use your digits to tickle, squeeze and rub while your tongue is getting busy.

Sun Sign Gemini: Role With It

Geminis are multifaceted individuals, and they love nothing more than to bring different sides of their personality to the fore with a bit of sexy role play. It's a fun and seductive way for them to explore their fantasies and connect with their partner about theirs. The great thing about this is that it needn't be restricted to the bedroom. You could meet up on a date somewhere, dressed in character, or start the foreplay early in the day in anticipation of some evening action with some in-character texts. You can even try different accents, if that's your thing – whatever makes you feel hot and seductive and opens up a new side of yourself for exploration.

Rising Sign Gemini: Split Missionary

Rising Geminis love getting people to open up – and this position translates that quality somewhat literally! They also love to bring new inspiration, and this position enhances an old favourite with a fun twist.

The passive partner lies on their back while the active partner gets on top – so far, so missionary. But in this version, the passive partner opens their legs in a wide V, as far as they will go. The active partner then penetrates and/or grinds against the passive partner. This allows the active partner to get really deep if penetrating, and is also great for combining penetration with clitoral stimulation. The close face-to-face positioning means you can kiss or whisper to each other as you build to a glorious climax.

Moon Sign Gemini:
The Column

This position can help dual-natured Gemini Moons to become more aligned with their partner. It's also a great option for a fast and furious quickie, and who doesn't love one of those?

This is a little bit like upright spooning, with both partners standing up straight and the active partner tucking in behind the passive partner. The key is to get snuggled in, really nice and close, so that your arms are entwined and can be used for leverage.

The active partner penetrates from behind – or they can reach around to stimulate their partner by hand – and controls the speed and rhythm with their thrusts as the passive partner arches their back and leans forward.

Cancer

Dates: 21 June–22 July

Zodiac symbol: The crab
Ruling planet: The Moon
Element: Water
Body hot spots: Breasts, stomach, womb

Sun Sign: Personality Overview

Just as their ruling planet, the Moon, has many phases, Cancerians have many changeable emotions. These empathic, intuitive souls are very nurturing, and they are often found in roles such as carer, cook and teacher. They care deeply and are hugely protective of the people they love, so they make for loyal partners. Like the crab of their sign, they may have a tough exterior that hides their soft and sensitive interior.

If you've ever seen a crab grasp something in their pincers, you'll have some idea of what it's like when a Cancerian latches on to something. They can be very determined, and once an idea has lodged with them, it can be very difficult to convince them to let go, even when it no longer serves them. In love, it can be hard for them to trust that everything will be okay and to let go of control. This trait can also show up as hoarding, with the homes of Cancerians featuring piles of books and trinkets they have collected along life's journey.

Love and Relationships

Cancerians can be shy at first. They are most at ease in a one-on-one situation, where they can form close bonds quite quickly. Kind and sensitive, they are usually drawn to those with the same qualities.

Crabs have a lot of love to give – lovers, relatives, children, pets and even house plants all flourish under their nurturing care. The flip side of this is that they can be oversensitive and are easily hurt by any perceived criticism. They crave security and to feel loved – if they don't receive this, they are prone to retreat into their shells until they feel safe enough to come out.

Cancers typically don't go in for one-night stands, as they need to be emotionally involved to enjoy sex. But once they've formed a connection, they go all in. Cancers are thoughtful, open and intuitive in bed, and super focused on their partner's satisfaction.

Cancers will thrive in relationships with Capricorn, Pisces and other Cancerians. They are best off staying away from Aquarius and Leo.

Rising Sign: Overview

Cancer Rising people can seem shy, insecure and super sensitive, especially in new environments and around new people. But give them time, and they will slowly emerge from their shell as they learn more about the situation. When it comes to love, Cancer Rising will provide comfort and security, turning any relationship into a sanctuary. Love needs to be there before they can really let go and enjoy sex, but rest assured, they have plenty of creativity to unleash.

Moon Sign: Overview

Moon in Cancer people tend to be very comfortable with their own feelings and feel responsible for the emotional well-being of others. Home and family are top priorities for these caring individuals. A romance with a Cancer Moon person is likely to be intense and attachment can occur quickly. Their overwhelming need is to feel secure. Once they feel this with you, they will shower you with love and affection that will make you never doubt their love.

Sun Sign Cancer: Missionary

Cancerians are nurturing, emotional and loving, and for them, sex is all about intimacy. Sometimes, simple is best. Tried and tested missionary takes the technicality out of sex and allows partners to focus on each other, gazing deeply into each other's eyes.

The passive partner lies on their back, while the active partner gets on top and either penetrates or grinds against the passive partner. The key here, for really feeling a connection, is to take things slow and steady. You can even stop every now and then, taking a break to kiss, look into each other's eyes or simply hold each other while the active partner is still inside.

Sun Sign Cancer:
Tickling the Tip of the Iceberg

If you really want to set your Cancer partner aglow, dedicate some serious foreplay time to their breasts and/or nipples.

Nipples are one of the top erogenous zones in the body, brimming with nerve endings that light up the brain the same way as when the genitals are stimulated. Here are some ways for you to show these small but powerful bits some love:

- Use your tongue to caress and flick the nipple and push it in with your tongue.

- Suck the nipple, then blow on it gently while it's still wet.

- Dribble some honey on the nipple and lick it off.

- Experiment with nipple clamps, or just give them a cheeky pinch.

Sun Sign Cancer:
Tummy Tingles

Like the soft underbelly of a crab, a Cancerian's
stomach is their most vulnerable spot. If they let
you touch it, then you know you have won their
trust. The stomach is not generally thought of as a
sexy part of the body, but there is something deeply
intimate about gently stroking, caressing or even
licking this area. It is strongly connected to health,
emotion and sensuality. For women, applying
pressure to the lower abdomen can also increase
sensation during orgasm.

Rising Sign Cancer:
The Flame

While they can be timid at first, once a Rising Cancer feels relaxed with a partner, they have a lot of energy and creativity to unleash. Looking a bit like a dirty dance move, this standing position ticks both boxes: it's athletic and presents a fun challenge.

Start this one by standing face to face with your partner. The passive partner brings their bent leg up in line with the active partner's hip, wrapping one arm around their neck for support and pulling their head down toward their chest.

The active partner grasps the passive partner's leg and leans in, kissing and teasing the passive partner's nipples (a Cancer hot spot) as they penetrate them (if desired).

Moon Sign Cancer: Dragon

Moon in Cancer people are always thinking about the emotional well-being of others and taking care of their needs. In a sexual partnership, they love to give their partners pleasure with oral sex, and this position provides a fun way for them to do exactly that.

The active partner sits back on their heels, facing their partner. The passive partner then lies down on their back and raises their bottom end up onto their partner's knees so that they are almost upside down. The passive partner spreads their legs, and the active partner can then dip their head down to give them oral pleasure, cradling the passive partner's bottom for support.

Leo

Dates: 23 July–22 August

Zodiac symbol: The lion
Ruling planet: The Sun
Element: Fire
Body hot spots: Heart, upper back, spine

Sun Sign: Personality Overview

There is no mistaking the fact that Leos are ruled by the Sun. These flamboyant, creative, proud souls light up and energize the people around them. Their love of laughter and fun can be unstoppably infectious. Nothing feels better to a Leo than being the centre of attention and getting people organized. While this may seem dramatic, it is more than compensated for by Leos' open and generous spirit. Known for their honesty and loyalty, they are great people to have in your corner, especially when times get tough.

They are usually very popular and have plenty of friends. Leos can be a little bit bossy toward the ones they care about, and in any relationship, they need to feel like they are the centre of the universe. That's because despite their boisterous exteriors, Leos are more easily hurt than most people might think. Constructive criticism can feel like a blow to their ego. But know this: to be loved by a Leo is to bathe in the glorious light of the Sun.

Love and Relationships

A lion in love is a happy lion, and they will want to shout it from the rooftops. If you're lucky enough to have a Leo as your partner, know that they will place you at the centre of their universe. Leos love to perform, and romance is a calling to do exactly that.

Leo is a fire sign, and you will no doubt feel the flames of their passion between the sheets. With their love for constant attention, you might assume that they would be selfish in bed, but while they certainly won't be shy about communicating their needs, they'll also go to great lengths to light you up inside. Leos thrive on feeling desired. Sexual tension is what gets them going – and they'll be keen to make it last as long as they can with some creative foreplay.

Leos' forever love could be an Aquarius, Libra or Sagittarius, but it's highly unlikely to be a Taurus or Capricorn.

Rising Sign: Overview

A Leo ascendant is rarely without a crowd of followers. Entertaining and showing off is in their blood, but they exude such generosity and warmth that it is easy to overlook their inflated egos. Natural-born organizers and leaders, they can come across as bossy at times, and yet they're people pleasers at heart. They live to give love, and sex is always fun and natural with them.

Moon Sign: Overview

Leo Moon types like to be in control and can be a tad dramatic in their efforts to achieve this. If you date one of these ardent souls, expect to be swept off your feet. But be aware: their dominant need is to receive approval, so expect to spend a lot of time telling them how wonderful they are. Your efforts will be rewarded. Folk with their Moon in Leo are very expressive when it comes to showing their feelings, and sex is the most natural and carefree way for them to do so.

Sun Sign Leo: Doggy Style

A tried and tested classic, this is one for anyone who loves to lose control and unleash some animalistic passion – and Leos love to do exactly that.

One of the great things about this position is that there are many different varieties, so it never need get boring. The basic idea is that the active partner stands up or kneels and penetrates or grinds against the passive partner from behind. The passive partner can be on all fours on the bed, lying on their stomach with a leg bent to elevate their torso, or even bent over a chair or other piece of furniture. Use your imagination and find what works best for you!

Finish with an after-sex spooning session once all that carnal desire is spent.

Sun Sign Leo: Rough and Ready

As the cat of the zodiac, lusty Leos love a bit of rough play between the sheets. It can bring out their animalistic nature. Here are some ideas to throw into your next lovemaking session to get your Leo purring:

- Lightly scrape your nails down their back (one of Leo's hot spots).

- Nibble their ears and neck or bite a little more firmly into their shoulder.

- Tug on their hair.

- Give them a cheeky slap on the bottom – or even a spanking if they're into that.

- Hold their wrists together and pin them down while you pleasure them.

Always check in with your partner when engaging in rough play. And don't be shy to switch things up and be on the receiving end.

Sun Sign Leo:
Sensual Back Massage

There's nothing more relaxing to get you in the mood for love than a sensual massage – and for Leos, whose backs are a hot spot of their anatomy, you can't go wrong with a back massage.

Perhaps light some candles and put on some sultry music. Invite your Leo lover to lie face down naked on the bed, with a pillow to rest their head on. Warm a few drops of massage oil in your hands. Start with a series of smooth, rhythmic strokes, using your palms to warm up the muscles. Beginning at the lower back, make circular motions with your hands, moving slowly up and pressing more firmly with your thumbs. Move across the shoulders and the upper arms, using less pressure as you move downward.

It's up to you whether you finish with a happy ending.

Rising Sign Leo:
The Spider Web

Warm-hearted Leo ascendants are natural lovers, who like nothing more than getting close with their partner. This intimate position allows for heart-to-heart contact, guaranteed to leave any Leo feeling warm and fuzzy inside.

Lie down, side by side, facing one another on the bed. Move right in and scissor your legs into an interlocked position. From here, the active partner can penetrate the passive partner deeply, or it's also perfect for hot and heavy frottage. Hold on tight to heighten leverage and friction. In your intimate embrace, you can kiss, nibble and lick each other's head, neck and nipples to your hearts' content. Try gyrating your hips in circular motions to build toward an explosive finish.

Moon Sign Leo: Supernova

Moon in Leo folk love to be in control. This position will answer their deep desire for dominance while treating their partner to an out-of-this-world experience.

The passive partner lies on their back on the bed with their head near to the edge. The active partner then straddles them "cowgirl/cowboy" style. Whether using penetration or grinding, the active partner rocks back and forth, building up a rhythm until both partners are close to the edge.

Before you both climax, the active partner stops rocking, shifts their weight into their knees and holds on to their partner's torso to move them right to the edge of the bed, so that their head, shoulders and arms hang down to the floor. The active partner resumes rocking until both partners orgasm – which, for the passive partner with the blood rushing to their head, will be an enhanced, intense experience.

Virgo

Dates: 23 August–22 September

Zodiac symbol: The virgin
Ruling planet: Mercury
Element: Earth
Body hot spots: Stomach, waist

Sun Sign: Personality Overview

Busy, busy, busy: Virgos always have something to do. These neat, capable characters like to keep on top of things. They have supreme organizational skills, so if you ever need help sorting out a mess, you'll want them around. Their desire for everything to be tidy can stray into perfectionism – not just when it comes to themselves but also when giving advice to others. This can come across as critical, but really, they're just trying to help.

Virgos can be somewhat shy at first. It can take a while for them to warm up, but once they do, it can be hard to get a word in edgeways – thanks to their ruling planet, chatty Mercury. Rest assured, they are listening, though, and will often remember little details such as things you like. They are also a lot of fun, and can always be relied upon for witty conversation and good times. When it comes to romance, they are patient, kind and thoughtful, though sometimes they need reminding to relax and not sweat the small stuff.

Love and Relationships

When it comes to matters of the heart, modest Virgos can be a little reserved at first and struggle to show their vulnerable side. It can take some time to earn their trust, but once they feel appreciated and secure within a relationship, they can truly blossom. They are incredibly thoughtful and attentive and will pick up on every small detail of their partner's behaviour. Of course, this is rather endearing, but it can also feel a little intense at times.

Virgos prefer stable relationships to short flings and need to feel emotional connection in order to fully enjoy sex. With their superb attention to detail, Virgos make thorough lovers. They have a unique ability to pinpoint a partner's pleasure spots, preferences and peccadilloes and target these with almost scientific precision. Sometimes, though, they do need reminding to let go and have some spontaneous fun.

Virgos get along well with Capricorn, Taurus and Pisces, but when it comes to Aries and Leo, things can get tense.

Rising Sign: Overview

Kind-hearted Virgo ascendants always seems to know how to make people feel better and love to be of practical help. In fact, they would benefit from more of their own compassion at times. They are skilled at restoring order from chaos and can break down any problem into easier-to-manage parts. When faced with a new love match, they can spend a lot of time analyzing before surrendering to it, but once they do, they do so wholeheartedly.

Moon Sign: Overview

Moon in Virgo people can be quite timid emotionally. They tend to find comfort in working through their feelings in a logical way. And if they have a crush on you, don't hold your breath for them to admit it. Once in a relationship, they are very affectionate, though they can struggle to express their emotions – and their perfectionist tendencies may lead them to try to fix yours. This conscientiousness often finds its way into the bedroom, which can feel restrictive, but if you let yourself go with it, it can be very rewarding.

Sun Sign Virgo: The Torch

You will both need focus and core strength to maintain this position, which is great for Virgos, because it offers them a challenge and helps to get them out of their heads.

The active partner sits back on their heels in a wide-legged kneeling position. The passive partner sits in the active partner's lap and – here comes the tricky part – puts their legs up onto the active partner's shoulders. The passive partner hugs the active partner's shoulders and throws back their head, while the active partner puts their arms around their back for support.

The active partner then controls the rhythm and pace, building toward a brilliant and blinding finish.

Sun Sign Virgo: Lip-Licking Good

With their famous attention to detail and desire to get things right, Virgo has a bit of a reputation for being prissy, but that couldn't be further from the truth: they are just as horny as any other zodiac sign. Virgos believe that sex is beautiful and that it's worth taking the time to build up to the action. Because of this, they love to start with some oral sex before the main act – and they are usually pretty expert at it. They will need little encouragement to get down and dirty with their tongue, but to give them a treat, you could try adding a flavoured lube to the mix or drizzle some honey on your stomach for them to lick off.

Sun Sign Virgo:
Indulging the Senses

As earth signs, Virgos are particularly tuned in to the senses, and they love indulging in all of them during sex. One of the best ways of heightening certain sensations is to remove other sensations, so that the mind hones in on what remains. To focus your partner on the sensations of touch, taste or smell, remove other stimuli by tying a blindfold around their eyes or dimming the lights and putting noise-cancelling headphones over their ears. Now try some of the following to awaken their senses:

- Waft a handkerchief imbued with aromatherapy oil under their nose.

- Smear chocolate on your skin and direct them to lick it off.

- Tickle their skin with a feather.

- Circle their nipple with an ice cube.

Rising Sign Virgo: Lazy Dog

Virgo ascendants are always busy helping others and solving problems, using their superior analytical skills. Sometimes, though, they need to just let go and surrender to the moment and be on the receiving end for a change. This position will help them to do just that. With maximum close contact, it also amplifies intimacy.

The passive partner lies on their front, arms bent at the elbows. They spread their legs wide apart and bend one at the knee. The active partner then lies on top, covering the passive partner with their entire body and penetrates or grinds from behind. The active partner can prop themselves up onto their hands to take some of the weight off if needed. Now all the passive partner needs to do is let go and enjoy the ride.

Moon Sign Virgo: The Aphrodite

There is nothing like being scooped up in the arms of your lover to make you feel on top of the world. Emotionally timid Virgo Moons will feel supported and loved in this sensual position, which is a little bit like an elegant side-saddle cowgirl/cowboy.

The active partner sits with their legs stretched out in front of them, while the passive partner sits on top, facing to the side. The active partner cradles the passive partner in their arms, supporting them with one arm beneath their thighs and the other around their back. You can work together to control the pace and rhythm, while the intimacy of the hold means that you can easily kiss and caress each other throughout.

Libra

Dates: 23 September–22 October

Zodiac symbol: The scales
Ruling planet: Venus
Element: Air
Body hot spots: Lower back, glutes

Sun Sign: Personality Overview

As the sign that takes the scales as its symbol, for Libra, balance and harmony are everything. They are constantly striving for justice and equality, whether that's in their personal connections or on a wider level in society. As an air sign, they crave intellectual stimulation, and love nothing more than discussing a good book with friends. They find it hard to make decisions and love to have someone to bounce ideas back and forth with.

Easy-going, charming and gregarious, Librans work best when surrounded by people and prefer not to spend too much time alone. Thanks to their tact and diplomacy, they can get along with almost anybody, and are often social chameleons, flitting between various groups.

Ruled by beauty-loving Venus, Librans are often skilled at crafts, love travelling to beautiful places and have a refined taste in art and music.

Romance and relationships are important to the typical Libra, meaning that their expectations of their partners can be high, but their sense of fairness means they are easy to get along with.

Love and Relationships

Librans are great romantics at heart – this should come as no surprise, since Libra is the zodiac sign most associated with love and relationships (hello, ruling planet Venus). However, sometimes they can fall foul of being in love with the *idea* of love. Nevertheless, they will treat the object of their affections with great warmth and emotion. They can get caught up in always functioning as a unit and may sometimes need a gentle reminder that a couple is formed of two independent human beings.

Libras are incurable flirts, so it can be difficult for others to know whether they are really interested. For Librans, relationships are just another way of finding balance in life, so they tend to be constantly attached. They can be sweet, romantic and generous in bed. Balance comes into play again here: Librans are consistent and fair when it comes to both giving and receiving satisfaction.

Paired with Aries, Gemini or Taurus, a Libra will flourish in love, but if they're teamed up with a Sagittarius or Virgo, things can quickly go downhill.

Rising Sign: Overview

Libra ascendant folk are often very easy on the eye, and they dislike ugliness, endeavouring always to make themselves and their surroundings attractive. They are charming, well-mannered and sociable, and like to make others feel at ease. This extends to the sphere of love: Libra ascendants magnetically attract lovers, and they will do whatever they can to keep them satisfied.

Moon Sign: Overview

Moon in Libra people rely heavily on others, often adopting the thoughts and feelings of those closest to them as their own. They detest confrontation and will do whatever it takes to keep the peace. They have a deep need for relationships and will always be fair and consider their partner's views and needs, sometimes at their own expense. They flourish best in love with someone who will consider their needs just as well, so remember to tell your Moon in Libra lover how much you appreciate their commitment to your relationship.

Sun Sign Libra:
Side 69

Libras are all about harmony and balance, so it's no surprise that in bed they love to give as much as they receive. This position allows them to do both in equal measure, taking a classic and turning it on its side for maximum pleasure in a relaxed pose.

One partner lies on their side, with their shoulder on a pillow, their arm outstretched and their legs half bent. The other partner then takes up the same position, facing their partner so that they are head to toe – or, rather, mouth to genitals. The partners then mutually pleasure each other – and that's pretty much all there is to it.

Remember to take your time with this one, and use your free arm to stroke, rub and caress your lover in this intimate pose.

Sun Sign Libra:
All About the Booty

The main Libran body hot spots are their lower back and bottom, so if you really want to please them, pay attention to these oft-neglected areas. A few ideas to try are:

- A sensual lower back massage.

- Tickling their lower back and bottom with a feather.

- Give the booty a good old squeeze, making sure to get your fingertips in the extra-sensitive cleft (the crack).

- Deliver a few light spanks – aimed right on the bottom swell of the cheeks for maximum eroticism.

- Part those cheeks and push them back together – try it, you'll be surprised how satisfying it is.

Sun Sign Libra: Phone Sex

As an air sign, Libra doesn't always need to be physical – for them, a lot of the fun happens in the brain. And what better way to get to know a Libran's most intimate, dirty thoughts than by engaging in a bit of cheeky phone sex with them.

Start with a slow burn by texting throughout the day. Give them a sneak peak of your filthiest fantasies and find out what gets them hot. Let them know exactly what you'd like to do with them later, and where and how.

If you are separated by distance, make a date for a steamy call when you're both in a private place. Describe in detail what you'd be doing to them if they were there in your arms – and what you're doing to yourself right now.

Rising Sign Libra:
Bandoleer

A Libra ascendant lover will do whatever it takes to keep their partner satisfied. This position combines comfort with deep penetration for a long, lingering ride you won't be forgetting any time soon.

The passive partner lies on their back, their head supported by a pillow. The active partner kneels in front and the passive partner puts their feet up on their partner's chest, resting their thighs and bottom on the active partner's thighs. Or they can support the small of their back with pillows. The active partner slowly enters and gradually builds up to deeper, harder penetration. If penetration is not your thing, swap it for manual stimulation – the passive partner will be in prime position for full access.

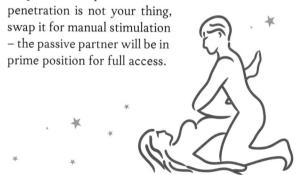

Moon Sign Libra:
Kneeling Congress

Moon in Libra folk are conscientious about tending to their partner's needs and thrive with a partner who will tend just as well to theirs. This position is perfect to ensure both partners get their needs met and fosters intimacy. Facing each other, you will be able to look deep into each other's eyes, and your sensitivity will be heightened as your bodies brush and press together.

The two partners kneel up in front of each other. The active partner keeps their legs together, while the passive partner straddles them and wraps their arms around the active partner's neck. The active partner can either penetrate, or both partners can touch using manual stimulation in a slow, gentle rhythm, building to an ecstatic release.

Scorpio

Dates: 23 October–21 November

Zodiac symbol: The scorpion
Ruling planet: Pluto
Element: Water
Body hot spots: Genitals, eyes, neck

Sun Sign: Personality Overview

Ruled by Pluto, if Scorpios have one key quality associated with them, it is their intensity. These deep characters have great emotional and physical energy, for which they need to find a positive outlet.

When it comes to money, they are very prudent; while at work, they enjoy getting stuck into a challenge – and the more daunting, the better. They are very curious about what makes people tick and love to collect friends from various walks of life, thriving on the different perspectives. Deeply intuitive, they can have an uncanny empathy with people, but beware: once offended or hurt, they can resort to power games, putting their infamous "stinger" into action.

In romance they can be demanding, and while secretive themselves, they can constantly scrutinize their partners, which can be a little hard to bear. And yet, a bond with a Scorpio can be deeply rewarding thanks to their intuition, insight and loyalty. If only Scorpios could let down their guard and be vulnerable, things might be a little easier all round.

Love and Relationships

Scorpio is here and things are about to get saucy. It's not for nothing that Scorpio has the reputation of the dynamo of the zodiac. These sexy scorpions only know one way to love: with intense passion. Their reputation precedes them, and they are never short of willing partners – and they never tend to get a bad review, either. The trouble is, they can struggle to move past the purely physical side of a relationship to something deeper. They tend to disguise their real feelings, only opening up if they are with a partner that they feel they can truly trust. Deep down, what they really want is someone who isn't frightened of real intimacy, someone they can share their deepest secrets and experiences with.

Put Scorpio with another Scorpio, a Cancer or a Taurus and watch the sparks sizzle; match them with a Leo or Gemini and you'll soon see any flames fizzle out.

Rising Sign: Overview

There are few who can resist the power of Scorpio Rising's intense gaze. These individuals can seem enigmatic and difficult to get to know. They hold great power, something that others cannot fail to notice. And that power can incite an irresistible danger when it comes to love and sex. Scorpio Rising is no stranger to obsession. For them, love is forever. They are loyal, fiercely protective and capable of great emotional courage.

Moon Sign: Overview

Moon in Scorpio people are deep and capable of intense emotional involvement, though they might not always show it. They usually keep their feelings hidden and find it hard to trust others. But once you find your way into their heart, you will be rewarded with deep loyalty and love. Above all, they crave depth. It is nearly impossible to avoid emotional entanglement if the relationship turns sexual. And with the Moon in Scorpio, it will always be deeply sexual.

Sun Sign Scorpio:
The Erotic V

This challenging position requires a fair bit of stability and core strength. If any star sign has the skills to do it, it's Scorpio, who never shies away from a challenge in the bedroom and likes to keep things interesting. Just remember to limber up first.

The passive partner sits at the edge of a table or other firm surface. The active partner stands in front and the passive partner raises their legs and rests them against the active partner's shoulders. The passive partner can wrap their arms around the active partner's neck, while the active partner can hold on firmly to the passive partner's bottom while they enter them. This position lets you go deep, and the angle lends itself to a satisfying rocking motion that should see you both to the finish line.

Sun Sign Scorpio:
Mirror, Mirror on the Ceiling

Scorpios' dedication to sex is almost academic – they are willing to try most things, if they haven't already, and will go the extra mile to perfect their technique and ensure their partner is having a good time. Plus, they are known for being just the teensiest bit self-admiring – which is why installing a mirror in the bedroom can only be a good thing. Whether you invest in a full-length freestanding mirror or go the whole hog and get one fitted on the ceiling, the main objective is to be able to watch yourselves as the fun unfolds. Scorpio will love checking you out from different angles... and won't mind checking themselves out too. So go ahead, unleash your inner exhibitionist and show them a good time.

Sun Sign Scorpio: Anywhere But Bed

Scorpios are known for their adventurousness between the sheets… and out of them. They love nothing more than to get out in the field, as it were, and try different locations around the house and beyond. Here are a few ideas for you to try together:

- Scorpios love to have sex standing up, so why not try up against the wall or the kitchen counter.

- Having sex in water is a huge turn-on for Scorpios, so next time you're having a shower, why not invite them in – or go for a midnight skinny dip in a secluded spot together?

- Have you ever done it in the woods? The primal feeling of getting down and dirty among nature is unparalleled, so long as you don't get spotted by passing joggers!

Rising Sign Scorpio: The Ape

Welcome to the jungle. And who better to guide you through it than sexually adept Scorpio Rising. This advanced animalistic position will have you howling their name and begging for more.

The active partner will need strength, stamina, flexibility and balance here. But it will be worth it, as it allows for deep penetration that paves the way for intense pleasure.

The passive partner lies on their back – better on a firm surface such as the floor – with their knees up to their chest. The active partner sits on the passive partner, facing away, resting their back on their partner's feet, as the passive partner penetrates or grinds against them. The active partner can control the rhythm and speed you both go at by moving up and down. For extra support, they can reach for the passive partner's wrists.

Moon Sign Scorpio: The Rowing Boat

Those born with the Moon in Scorpio crave deep emotional and sexual connection. This seated position provides the framework for both, at the same time as testing Moon in Scorpio's adept bedroom skills. For while it may look simple, it's actually not all that easy to pull off effectively.

The active partner lies down, while the passive partner straddles them and penetrates them, if desired. Once in position, the passive partner then pulls the active partner up into a seated position, with their knees bent and supported by their partner's arms. The active partner places their hands under the passive partner's bottom to help control penetration and from here, you can "row" your way to orgasm.

Sagittarius

Dates: 22 November–21 December

Zodiac symbol: The archer
Ruling planet: Jupiter
Element: Fire
Body hot spots: Hips, thighs

Sun Sign: Personality Overview

If there is one sign in the zodiac synonymous with freedom, it's Sagittarius. These wild spirits love adventure and don't let anything hold them back – even little inconveniences like, say, not having enough money in the bank to fund a trip.

They thrive on challenges, no matter how daunting, and their infectious enthusiasm usually helps to see them through. Ruled by optimistic Jupiter, they rarely let a setback get them down for long. They aren't too interested in rules and regulations, which they find unnecessary and boring.

Sagittarians are frank, honest and funny, making them great company – even if they are occasionally a bit inappropriate. They tend to be very direct about what they really think or feel, a refreshing trait that keeps things interesting.

They loathe the idea of being stifled or restricted, so in a relationship they really need someone open-minded who will understand their need to keep moving and will bring their own inspiration to the table. If things aren't kept fresh, they can lose interest and drift away to find their next romantic adventure.

Love and Relationships

Sagittarians have a bit of a reputation for being hard to tie down. And no wonder, since they are so independent. They usually want space rather than closeness, so when they do fall in love with someone, they can find it overwhelming and unbalancing. If they can relax and see their new relationship as an adventure in its own right, one in which they will make exciting discoveries about themselves and their partner, they will enter into it with their trademark openheartedness and enthusiasm.

In matters of sex, their carefree, playful nature makes them ideal partners for a fling or one-night stand. But they also have a lot to bring to the bedroom in a long-term relationship. Their enthusiasm for experimentation helps to keep things fresh, whether that's by coming up with inventive ideas for foreplay or introducing sex toys into the mix.

Sagittarius should look out for a Leo, Libra or Aries to hold on to, and should let Capricorn and Taurus go.

Rising Sign: Overview

To Sagittarius ascendants, life is a game – and they usually come out winning. These larger-than-life types enjoy competition and sport and get very restless if life becomes too predictable. They approach everything as an adventure, including love. And it's never the destination that matters, but rather the fun you can have along the way. They thrive best with a partner who is confident enough to set them free once in a while. Once they're done exploring, they will always come back for true love.

Moon Sign: Overview

Sagittarius Moons wear their hearts on their sleeve. They live by the concept that actions speak louder than words and don't dwell on their emotions for long. These freedom lovers don't like to feel tied down and aren't sentimental, though they are warm and loving in their own way. Their propensity for positivity may lead them to put their partner and their relationship on a pedestal. They are philosophers at heart and need their lover to listen to and respect their opinions and beliefs.

Sun Sign Sagittarius: Relaxed Arch

Sagittarians are always down for experimentation in the bedroom, and this position presents the opportunity to see things from a fresh perspective. It takes a bit of flexibility and comes from the Tantric sex practice, opening up a new horizon for curious Sagittarians to explore.

The active partner sits upright on the bed or floor with their legs straight out in front. The passive partner sits on the active partner's lap, facing them, allowing for penetration. The passive partner can then gradually arch their back until they can rest their head between their partner's legs and grab hold of their feet.

Cradling the passive partner's lower back, the active partner controls the rhythm and speed. It is thought that penetration from this angle targets the G-spot.

Sun Sign Sagittarius: Don't Stop There

The thighs are Sagittarians' number one hot spot. If you really want to drive them wild, treat your Sagittarian partner to an erotic thigh massage. Have your partner lie down on the bed on their back. Starting at the knee, make circular rubbing strokes and work your way up the legs until you are almost at the top. Repeat, stopping a bit higher each time and inching closer to their genitals, eventually grazing them lightly with your fingertips on each circular motion at the top. Then move away and start at the knee again. This teasing routine is bound to simultaneously relax your partner and have them begging for more.

Sun Sign Sagittarius: Play Time

If there is one thing guaranteed to get a Sagittarian partner intrigued, it's adding some sex toys into the mix – from vibrators to anal beads. Here are some ideas to try:

- Sex toys don't only have to be used on the genitals. Experiment with other areas, for example holding a vibrator against your nipples or running a smooth dildo down your partner's back.

- Use a vibrator to stimulate yourself during penetration.

- Go remote. Some sex gadgets come with a remote and can be operated from afar. Handing over control to your partner is pretty hot.

- Play with temperature. Some toys retain temperature when run under warm water or placed in the fridge.

Rising Sign Sagittarius: Crossed Keys

This position is perfect for adventurous Sagittarius ascendants, because you can do it in various locations – a table, the kitchen counter, maybe even in an aeroplane bathroom.

The active partner stands, while the passive partner lies on their back on the flat surface so that their bottom is at hip height for the active partner. They then put their legs in the air, crossing them at the knees or ankles.

The active partner then penetrates from their standing position, or uses manual stimulation, while holding the passive partner's legs up against their body. As they thrust, they cross and uncross the passive partner's legs, the squeezing action contributing to the passive partner's orgasm.

Moon Sign Sagittarius: Barberry

Moon in Sagittarius folk are lovers of freedom and flexibility, so they might just enjoy the yoga-like element of this bendy pose. Plus, being unsentimental souls, they won't be perturbed by the lack of eye contact.

The passive partner lies on a pillow on the bed with legs bent at the knees, their hands reaching back to grasp their feet and their head raised. For the yogis out there – it's like the bow pose.

The active partner kneels between the passive partner's legs, leans forward and grasps their bottom as they enter them from behind, controlling the rhythm and pace to send the passive partner into sweet bliss.

Capricorn

Dates: 22 December–19 January

Zodiac symbol: The goat
Ruling planet: Saturn
Element: Earth
Body hot spots: Bones, knees, teeth

Sun Sign: Personality Overview

Picture a mountain goat on a rocky precipice. Calm, cool and determined, they pick their way carefully along the edge, looking ahead to plan each next step. That pretty much sums up your typical Capricorn, who won't be rushed into anything – and isn't fazed by challenging circumstances. With their strong and steady approach, they are often winners, though you will never hear them brag about it.

Ruled by serious Saturn, Capricorns can come across as a little bit distant, and they are experts at keeping their emotions in check. But if you can break through this tough exterior, you will discover a warm and loyal soul. And when they feel at ease and start to loosen up, they will unleash their wicked sense of humour.

Capricorns keep small circles, preferring quality over quantity, and are super supportive of their friends and loved ones. They love creating comfortable, luxurious homes, and living well is important to them. Capricorns are highly self-aware, and they get what makes other people tick, too, making them reliable, understanding romantic partners.

Love and Relationships

Given their measured approach to all other aspects of life, it makes sense that Capricorns are not impulsive when it comes to love. They may come across as picky, but in fact they are only so careful about who they choose to date because once they do make a commitment, they will take it very seriously and give it their all. They can also seem aloof at times, but this is only because they are a little bit shy when it comes to matters of the heart. In fact, they can find it hard to open up about their emotions and if they are hurt, they may never admit it.

The goat of the zodiac is very horny, and once they feel comfortable with a person, they are an enthusiastic lover. Sensitive and sensual in bed, they apply their trademark careful efficiency to sex and are willing to put in the time and effort to truly satisfy their partner.

Capricorns would do well to choose Virgo, Cancer or Pisces as a love match, and avoid Gemini and Leo.

Rising Sign: Overview

Shy and serious, Capricorn Rising is a responsible soul. This can be perceived as weak and a bit dull – all work and no play. And yet, Capricorn Rising's quiet ambition and willpower often sees them scaling the ladder of success one sure step at a time. They often apply this approach to relationships, too, carefully constructing the foundations of a love that will last and taking sex just as seriously. Sometimes, though, they do need a friendly reminder that dating is meant to be fun.

Moon Sign: Overview

The Moon in Capricorn brings out an emotionally cool aspect. And yet these characters take emotional matters very seriously, even if they don't show it at first. They are not risk takers and will weigh things up carefully before committing to anything. They take love very seriously and don't mess with other people's hearts. It may take them a while to warm up sexually, but once they get going, there is no stopping these lusty beings. If you are in any doubt of their feelings for you, those doubts will be quelled once you get between the sheets.

Sun Sign Capricorn:
Up Against a Wall

Strong and steady Capricorn will adapt well to this position, which presents a challenge with its need for core strength and stability.

The active partner stands and lifts the passive partner, who wraps their legs around the active partner's waist, pressing the passive partner's back up against a wall. The active partner can then penetrate or grind against the passive partner while standing.

If the passive partner's legs are well secured around the active partner's waist, the active partner should be able to pin the passive partner's arms against the wall for an extra edge of power play and dominance, which is sure to be especially exciting for Capricorn.

Sun Sign Capricorn: Naughty Knees

You may not think of knees as inherently sexy, but pay some attention to your Capricorn's knees and you will soon see this part of the anatomy in a different light.

The soft spot behind the knee is one of the body's key erogenous zones, thanks to its nerve-rich sensitivity. Being touched behind the knee also feels like a novelty, because it's not somewhere that anyone would normally touch.

Try gently touching your Capricorn partner behind the knees while they stand in front of you. Give them a mini massage there, alternating between deep pressure and a tickle. To really drive them crazy, make slow strokes up from the back of the knees toward the top of the leg.

Sun Sign Capricorn: Love Ties

Capricorn is ruled by Saturn, the planet associated with rules, regulations and structure. So don't be too surprised if your Capricorn partner enjoys playing with power and control in the bedroom and, more specifically, being tied up or tying you up.

You don't need to go full-on *Fifty Shades of Grey* to introduce this kink to your bedroom repertoire, and neither do you have to fork out on lots of expensive equipment and toys. Start simple, with a soft silk scarf as a blindfold or restraint to tie your partner's hands together or to the bedstead.

Communication is key. Make sure you let each other know what you are comfortable with. Above all, enjoy the delicious sensation of your partner pleasuring you while there is nothing you can do to stop them.

Rising Sign Capricorn: Coital Alignment Technique (CAT)

Capricorn Rising are shy, careful and practical at heart, so they may enjoy the precision of this scientifically documented technique. If you or your partner has a vagina – this one is for you.

American psychotherapist Edward Eichel first defined this position in 1988, writing in the *Journal of Sex and Marital Therapy*. It is intended specifically to allow for effective stimulation of the clitoris during intercourse, to give the partner with a clitoris... well, a jolly good orgasm.

The active partner lies above the passive partner, moving up until the penis or strap-on dildo is pointing down, so that the top of the penis presses against the clitoris during penetration. The partners begin to move their pelvises, with the passive partner rocking upward and the active partner stroking downward, building to an orgasmic peak.

Moon Sign Capricorn:
Hot Seat

Moon in Capricorn folk are careful souls and not prone to risk taking, so they will no doubt enjoy being in control as the passive partner in this saucy seated pose.

The active partner sits on the edge of a bed. Facing away from the active partner, the passive partner then lowers themselves down into a seated position on the active partner's lap, with the active partner sliding inside them, if penetration is being used. Alternatively, this can work just as well with the partner who is seated on the bed reaching around to give the passive partner manual stimulation. The narrow stance makes for more sensation, and the passive partner can adjust the pace to their liking. They can also reach down between their legs to stimulate the active partner if desired.

Aquarius

Dates: 20 January–18 February

Zodiac symbol: The water carrier
Ruling planet: Uranus
Element: Air
Body hot spots: Ankles, calves, shins

Sun Sign: Personality Overview

Meet Aquarius, the wild child of the zodiac. With rebellious Uranus as their ruling planet, it's hardly surprising that these quirky characters can be a little bit... out there.

Aquarians are also extremely friendly and are able to relate to many different types of people. These curious souls have so many questions when they first meet a person, which can be rather endearing. However, it can be hard for them to connect with others on a deeper level, and they tend to try to rationalize or explain emotions intellectually. They can come across as cold, but they just hold their emotions in more than most.

The symbol of the water bearer represents the gifts of truth and pure intentions that Aquarians bring to the world. They are very upfront and direct.

Aquarians are intelligent beings who excel at careers in engineering and science, combining their inventive side with their analytical powers to create innovative solutions. Often called the humanitarians of the zodiac, they want to save the world – and they have the smarts to do it.

Love and Relationships

Aquarians rebel against traditional roles and their love lives can err on the eccentric and experimental side. They are fiercely independent individuals, and they need a partner who can allow them space to grow. So, if you date an Aquarius, don't be surprised if, every now and then, they disappear off for some alone time: they need it to recharge.

Having an intellectual connection is super important to them, and they are best suited to someone who can also be their best friend. Once they have this, they make for wise and exciting partners. They are also very loyal in love. Being with one person who adores them gives these forward-thinking lovers the freedom to be open and rebellious in bed. They will try anything (at least) once! They can be overly focused on the physical, though, and may need reminding to focus more on the emotional side of things in bed.

Aquarians can find their heart's true desire with Virgo, Cancer or Pisces, but they may find disappointment with Gemini or Leo.

Rising Sign: Overview

Unconventional Aquarius Rising will bring fresh perspectives and unexpected solutions to problems. They're just built differently and experience the world in their own unique way. They often rebel against the norm and are keen advocates of social justice. When it comes to love and sex, they can be somewhat unpredictable. On the one hand, they crave the structure of a relationship, yet on the other, they resist "rules". They need a sexually progressive partner who can appreciate their need for individuality.

Moon Sign: Overview

A Moon in Aquarius person will have the charisma guaranteed to attract your attention. But they don't show warmth and passion openly, and so these intriguing creatures may seem rather hard to get close to. They tend to intellectualize their feelings and keep them in check on a one-to-one basis, with much of their energy going into efforts to make the world a better place. With their open-minded approach to life, they are most likely to be involved in an unconventional relationship.

Sun Sign Aquarius:
Aerial Dancer

Rebellious Aquarius is bound to love this daring standing position, and its "aerial" aspect will appeal to their air sign nature. It requires a fair amount of strength and concentration from both partners, but if you get it right, it will send you both to heaven.

The active partner stands upright, supporting the passive partner's bottom with their hands. The passive partner wraps their legs around the active partner to secure themselves in place. The active partner penetrates or grinds, rocking and bouncing the passive partner until they both reach cloud nine.

If this pose is too strong and you want to add a bit of extra support, try the Raised Dancer, which looks the same but has a bench positioned behind the active partner's legs for the passive partner to rest their feet on.

Sun Sign Aquarius:
Pre-Game Fun

Aquarians love to have fun, and when it comes to sex, a big part of that comes from foreplay. An Aquarian lover will want to feel closeness, to explore every bit of you – and for you to explore every bit of them. Here are some tips for making the prelude last:

- Get things started before you even get home – discreetly cop a feel of your partner's butt or sneakily stroke their leg.

- It may sound basic, but kissing with tongues is a proven way to create a deep connection. So pucker up and give your partner a long-lasting snog.

- For a bit of spontaneity, try some bed-wrestling. Tickle each other and pin each other down – anything goes as long as it's fun and sexy.

Sun Sign Aquarius: All Dressed Up

Eccentric Aquarians love nothing better than a good old dressing-up session – whether it's for a fancy-dress party or for a private cabaret at home. So go ahead and indulge your Aquarian lover's fantasies by donning a sexy costume and inviting them to do the same. Here are some ideas for items to include in your naughty dressing-up box:

- Masquerade-ball masks – team these with a full-length cloak and nothing underneath for the full *Eyes Wide Shut* effect.

- Little Red Riding Hood and the Wolf – take it in turns to be the baddie in this classic combo.

- A crown – maybe you don't fancy Prince William, but everyone likes to play at being prince or princess sometimes.

Rising Sign Aquarius: The Splitting Bamboo

Aquarius Rising people have a reputation for being unconventional and unpredictable – so it's not hard to imagine them whipping their partner's leg up in the air to get into this position. It's also much easier to do than it may look – "splitting" may sound off-putting, but it's very comfortable once you get in position and lends itself to lazy lovemaking sessions.

The passive partner lies on their back with one leg slightly bent out in front of them. The active partner straddles this leg and scoops up the passive partner's other leg, draping it over their shoulder. In this scissor-like shape, the active partner penetrates, or applies manual stimulation, or both, and starts up a gradual sliding rhythm to take both partners slowly across the finish line.

Moon Sign Aquarius: Magic Mountain

Moon in Aquarius folk can seem a little distant and overly intellectual at times. This position will allow them to loosen up and release their animalistic desires, while also bringing you up close and personal.

The passive partner crouches bent over a piece of furniture, the edge of the bed or a stack of pillows, placing their forearms flat on the surface to support their torso. The active partner then assumes a similar position while penetrating them from behind. It's a little bit like doggy style, but in this version, the partners' bodies are glued closely together, creating greater intimacy.

A fun tip for unconventional Moon in Aquarius folk to try: pop a vibrator between the furniture and the passive partner to give them an extra thrill.

Pisces

Dates: 19 February–20 March

Zodiac symbol: The fish
Ruling planet: Neptune
Element: Water
Body hot spots: Feet, toes

Sun Sign: Personality Overview

The Piscean symbol is of two fish swimming in opposite directions, while the sign's ruling planet is the ever-confusing and mystical Neptune. Those two things should give an idea of the fluidity and dual nature of this water sign.

Pisceans are equipped with practical artistic skills, yet prone to escape into the world of imagination. They have an innate sense of right and wrong, yet often get tempted by the path of least resistance.

Pisceans are compassionate, gentle and understanding, and will go out of their way to help those close to them. They are highly empathic and *feel* the suffering of the people they love. Because of this, they need to keep a firm grip on their own sense of identity and need frequent time away from others to come back to themselves.

As romantic partners, Pisces are poetic and have no hesitation in expressing their innermost feelings to the people they love. Unfortunately, they also have a tendency to ignore difficult situations, resulting in misunderstandings further down the line.

Love and Relationships

Pisceans are big romantics at heart. When they find that special someone, they are ready to give it their all. The only thing is, they are sometimes so caught up in fantasizing about romance that they forget to go out and actually find it.

Compassionate and emotional to a fault, these personalities make devoted partners. They are ready to woo, whisking you off on romantic dates and professing their love in their signature poetic style. Sometimes, though, they might just need a gentle nudge to bring them back down to reality and deal with the practicalities and responsibilities of being in an adult relationship.

Pisceans are naturally intuitive, and these powers come into play in the bedroom. These sensual lovers have a knack for finding all your pleasure spots. When they make love, they do so fully, losing themselves in the moment with you.

Pisceans can find their fairy-tale dream love with Virgo, Scorpio or Cancer, but an entanglement with an Aquarius or Libra is unlikely to lead to a happy ending.

Rising Sign: Overview

A Pisces Rising person is typically generous and sympathetic, and often very sensitive and sentimental. They have a huge capacity for compassion and sometimes this can be taken advantage of by others. Pisces ascendants need to be needed, but in a relationship, they must set strong boundaries to avoid losing themselves. In a good love match, their imagination can take sex to a whole new level.

Moon Sign: Overview

These sensitive souls are super tuned in to others' emotions and sometimes have trouble distinguishing them from their own. When unhappy they may have a tendency to find refuge in unhealthy habits; a better option would be for them to express their feelings creatively through music, art or writing. A Moon in Pisces person has an incredible imagination and an idealized approach to romance. They will put their lover on a pedestal and sometimes get lost in their dream version of reality. Being loved by a Moon in Pisces is like getting lost in a pink fluffy cloud – one you might never want to emerge from.

Sun Sign Pisces:
The Corkscrew

Somewhere between missionary and doggy style, this intimately entangled position will appeal to Pisces, who will love the chance to get full access to your pleasure spots. It might look complicated, but if you can get the set-up right, physically it's not too demanding as both partners are supported on the bed.

The passive partner lies on their back, rotating their pelvis and hips to one side. The active partner positions themselves kneeling between the passive partner's legs and penetrates or grinds. For more stability, the passive partner can wrap their legs around their partner's torso and the active partner can put one hand on the passive partner's waist, the other on their knee to get more leverage. You could also throw in a bit of manual stimulation to add to the fun.

Sun Sign Pisces: Frisky Feet

Pisces' prime hot spot is their feet, so you would be a fool to neglect this sensitive part of the body when trying to please your Piscean partner. Whether you are a foot fetishist or not, there is plenty of fun to be had with these oft-neglected extremities that are brimming with touch-sensitive nerve endings. Here are a few ideas to get you going:

- Tickle the base of the feet with a feather.

- Give your partner a sensual foot massage.

- Lavish some attention on the toes, gently kissing or sucking each one in turn.

- Invite them to try a foot job – whether giving or receiving.

Sun Sign Pisces:
Take it to the Edge

Intuitive, sensitive and emotional, Pisceans love to make things last when it comes to lovemaking. And nothing gives them a bigger thrill than "edging" – taking things almost to the point of no return and then pulling back at the last second.

The technique itself is simple in principle, but it requires good communication between partners. It's also a good way for you to learn about how long and what needs to happen before you both orgasm.

Start by stimulating your partner, either manually or orally. When you can see, or your partner signals, that they are about to orgasm, reduce or completely stop the stimulation. Wait for at least thirty seconds before starting again. It's up to you how long you tease them, and when they finally climax, it will be extra intense.

Rising Sign Pisces: Cradle

This romantic position is perfect for sensitive Pisces ascendant and will make the passive partner feel very supported and loved.

The active partner sits back on their heels, with their feet together and their knees apart. The passive partner then straddles the active partner, allowing them to penetrate or grind. Placing one arm around the active partner's neck and another on the bed behind them for support, the passive partner can lean back and really let go into the moment. The active partner can place both hands around their back for support, or just one hand and use the other to play with their nipples or add manual stimulation into the mix.

This can also work with the passive partner facing the other way, reverse cowgirl/cowboy style, but emotional Pisces ascendant may prefer the intimacy of face-to-face action.

Moon Sign Pisces:
Milk and Water Embrace

This steamy position has a gentleness to it that makes it ideal for dreamy Moon in Pisces lovers. Luckily, there is no actual milk or water required – well, unless you want to add them, of course!

The passive partner sits down on the edge of the bed or in an armless chair and the active partner sits on their lap, facing away. This is a slow and sultry pose, so start by letting the passive partner's hands roam over the active partner's body, caressing their skin and playing with their nipples.

When both partners are feeling ready for action, the active partner rises up slightly and then back down as the passive partner slides inside, if using penetration. The active partner rocks back and forth, while the passive partner continues to pleasure them with their hands.

Conclusion

We can learn so much about ourselves and the people around us through where we sit on the zodiac chart – from our career choices and style of humour to whether we run toward or away from adventure. As this book has shown, knowing your position in the night sky can also teach you a lot about your sexual self: the places you like to be touched, whether emotion or carnal lust is more important to you and what arouses you most.

We have come to the end of this tour of where the wonderful worlds of astrology and sex meet. Hopefully, as well as picking up some handy tips to take you and your partner to the dizzy heights of sensual bliss in the bedroom (and perhaps beyond), you will also feel more in touch with your own erogenous zones and between-the-sheets desires. Who knows, you may even have learned something new about yourself.

Whether you're a spontaneous Gemini, a sensual Cancer, or a quirky Aquarius, you will have added some new positions to your repertoire and had lots of sexy fun trying them out with your partner along the way. As Vātsyāyana, the author of the *Kama*

Sutra, once wrote, "Variety is necessary in love, so love is to be produced by means of variety."

And of course, the fun doesn't have to be over at the end of this book. There are many ways you can continue your journey of sexploration and learning about yourself through astrology – just take a look at some of the resources on the next page.

Resources

Books

Marion Williamson, *The Little Book of Astrology* (2017)

Liz Greene, *Astrology for Lovers* (1999)

Robert Hand, *Planets in Composite: Analyzing Human Relationships* (1997)

Carole Taylor, *Astrology: Using the Wisdom of the Stars in Your Everyday Life* (2018)

Gary Goldschneider, *The Astrology of You and Me: How to Understand and Improve Every Relationship in Your Life* (2018)

Websites

www.astrolibrary.org/category/astrology-calculators/

A free website for calculating your rising moon and sun signs.

www.astro.com

A wealth of information, including detailed relationship charts. You can also get a free birth chart and personalized daily horoscopes.

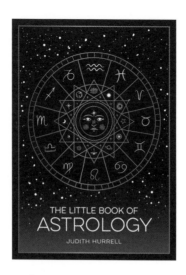

The Little Book of Astrology

Judith Hurrell

ISBN: 978-1-83799-392-5 ∗ Paperback

Embark on a journey of self-discovery and find your place in the cosmos with this spellbinding introduction to astrology. Whether you're curious about your own astrological profile or interested in understanding the cosmic messages in the world around you, this book is your gateway to the wisdom of the stars.

The Little Book of Sex Tips

Lexie Sutton

ISBN: 978-1-78783-272-5 ✳ Paperback

Do you want to know the secrets to a steamy and passionate, thrilling and fulfilling sex life? With moves to make your knees tremble and the bed rock, this little book is guaranteed to leave everyone in the bedroom (and beyond!) satisfied from head to toe.

Have you enjoyed this book?
If so, find us on Facebook at
Summersdale Publishers, on Twitter/X
at **@Summersdale** and on Instagram and
TikTok at **@summersdalebooks** and get
in touch. We'd love to hear from you!

www.summersdale.com

Image Credits

Sex position illustrations throughout by Agnes Graves
pp.9, 14, 23, 32, 41, 50, 59, 68, 77, 86, 95, 104, 113 –
zodiac symbols © Viktoriia Protsak/Shutterstock.com
pp.5, 19, 22, 27, 28, 32, 40, 47, 54, 56, 67, 73, 99, 118,
123 © ARTHA DESIGN STUDIO/Shutterstock.com
p.20 – blindfold © Valenty/Shutterstock.com
pp.38, 55, 92 – sex toys © fad82/Shutterstock.com
p.64 – lips © ValerieSerg/Shutterstock.com
p.65 – feather © YuummyBuum/Shutterstock.com
p.101 – tied hands © Yusup ahmad/Shutterstock.com
p.110 – high heel shoe © FlyIntoSpace/Shutterstock.com